A Very Special Thanks!

"What the Obama Care Affordable Health Insurance Act did for me and my family."

Written By Randolph M. Hirsch, The Golfing Accountant

Un-official spokesperson for the Obama Care Affordable Insurance Act and Blue Shield Covered California Health Insurance

WRITTEN ESPECIALLY FOR ALL SELF-EMPLOYED PEOPLE AND SMALL BUSINESS OWNERS ACROSS THIS GREAT COUNTRY OF OURS WHO CURRENTLY DON'T HAVE ANY HEALTH INSURANCE COVERAGE

CONTACT INFORMATION:

Moshe Publications, Inc.
Randolph M. Hirsch
Publisher and Editor
18375 Ventura Blvd, Suite # 526
Tarzana, CA 91356
Office: (818) 908-4083

http://www.MoshePublications.com

EMAIL: MoshePublications@gmail.com

Additional Copies of this book may be ordered
for Health Insurance Agents, Self employed
persons, Small business owners, Libraries,
Schools, Eye Doctors and for anyone without
proper Health Insurance coverage through
Moshe Publications, Inc.
at this website address:
http://www.A-Very-Special-Thanks.com

Books and DVDs by Randolph M. Hirsch

The Roy Yamaguchi Story: International Chef and founder of Roy's Hawaiian Fusion Restaurants. "The Ultimate Biography and color photo tour of Roy's Restaurants, including the six in Hawaii."

Molly and Dad's Grand Hawaii Adventure, A children's story and picture book

QUIT SMOKING: "How I finally did it after thirty years and you will too!"

Seth McFarlane: The Ultimate Trivia Guide and Biography of "The Family Guy."

A Very Special Thanks to the Obama Administration, Hillary Clinton, Blue Shield Health Insurance and Dr. Brad Elkins, Eye Surgeon. "What the Obama Care Affordable Insurance Act did for me and my family."
http://www.A-Very-Special-Thanks.com

Philip Seymour Hoffman: July1967- February 2014, The Complete Biography of a Great Actor, Memorabilia and Trivia Guide, April 2014 http://www.PhilipSeymour-Hoffman.com

Daniel Day-Lewis: Three Time Academy Award winner for Best Actor, the Ultimate Biography
http://www.DanielDay-LewisBook.com

The Blueprints Marketing Guide for Accountants, Tax Professionals and CPAs
http://www.BlueprintsMarketingGuide.com

Once In A Lifetime: "Just Go For It!" Feature length screenplay

"There's A Reason You're Here, Moshe" January 2014
www.RandolphMHirsch-MosheBook.com

Matthew McConaughey: Best Actor 2014! The Complete Unauthorized Color Biography and Trivia Guide, April 2014 (E-Book)

Making Kids Smile! A "How To Guide" for aspiring children's entertainers and performers
http://www.MakingKidsSmile.com

Randolph Hirsch's Ukraine Adventure, Travel Film DVD
http://www.RandolphHirsch-UkraineDVD.com

Randolph Hirsch Discovers Paris,
Travel Film DVD
http://www.RandolphHirsch-ParisDVD.com

Once In A Lifetime: Just Go For It! Short film
DVD version, (20 minutes) re-released in 2014
through On Demand Publishing

Cate Blanchett: Best Actress 2014! Color
Photo Biography and Trivia Guide (E-Book)

Mark Wahlberg: The Ultimate Biography
(Boogie Nights Series) May 2014 (E-Book)

Don Cheadle: The Ultimate Biography (Boogie
Nights Series) May 2014 (E-Book)

Julianne Moore: The Ultimate Biography
(Boogie Nights Series) May 2014 (E-Book)

William H. Macy: The Ultimate Biography
(Boogie Nights Series) May 2014 (E-Book)

Paul Thomas Anderson, Biography (Best
Director Series and Boogie Nights Series)
2014 (E-Book)

Burt Reynolds: The Ultimate Biography
(Boogie Nights Series) May 2014 (E-Book)

Heather Graham: The Ultimate Biography (Boogie Nights Series) May 2014 (E-Book)

Alfred Molina: The Complete Biography (Boogie Nights Series) May 2014 (E-Book)

John C. Reilly: The Complete Biography (Boogie Nights Series) May 2014 (E-Book)

THE ORDEAL: Scandal of the Decade – BEST TRUE STORY OF 2014

The Power of Social Media and SEO Marketing

How to Start Your Own Business in 30 Days or Less!

Kindle Gold Rush! Writing, publishing and selling your own E-Book on Kindle and Amazon

Twitter Power: Harness the immense power of Twitter to gain more customers and maximize your profits!

DEDICATED TO AND WRITTEN ESPECIALLY FOR ALL SELF EMPLOYED PEOPLE AND SMALL BUSINESS OWNERS ACROSS THE COUNTRY WHO CURRENTLY DON'T HAVE ANY HEALTH INSURANCE COVERAGE.

This book is specifically targeted to:

Self employed people across the country

Small business owners in the USA

Independent Insurance Agents all across this great country of ours wanting to offer the Obama Care Health plan and insurance coverage to their self employed clients

Any part-time or full-time employees who work for small business owners that don't offer any Health Insurance benefits

Golfers and Accountants Nationwide who are interested in Affordable Health Insurance coverage!

Anyone who has had a recent medical scare or procedure done, that didn't have any insurance -- and does not want to go through anything like that again --without proper Insurance!

Any person suffering from Cataracts disease or other illnesses, who cannot afford the necessary treatment or surgery and doesn't have proper Health Insurance coverage.

For special guest appearances, public speeches, phone interviews and book signings, contact Randy through Moshe Publications, Inc.
Toll-free: (855) 333-6897 or (818) 908-4083
MoshePublications@gmail.com

BOOK PROMOTION CAMPAIGN:

To kick off the worldwide book campaign for "A Very Special Thanks to the Obama Administration, Hillary Clinton, Blue Shield Insurance and Dr. Brad Elkins, Eye Surgeon" we're submitting a copy of this book to the following:

Hillary Clinton
Vice President Joe Biden and Mrs. Jill Biden
Oprah Winfrey, Harpo Studios, Inc.
President and Mrs. Obama
Amazon.com
Barnes and Noble
Kindle
Borders.com
Los Angeles Times, Book review
Chicago Times, Book review
New York Times, Book review
Google
Twitter
Facebook
The Jimmy Kimmel Show
The Ellen DeGeneres show
The Oprah Winfrey show
The Conan show
Late Night with Jimmy Fallon

The Late show with Craig Ferguson
Late Show with David Letterman
The Regis Philbin show
Charlie Rose
Tavis Smiley
Montel Williams show
Star Jones
Richard Bey show
Craig Kilborn show
The Sheila Gale show
The Today Show
Live with Kelly and Michael
Good Morning America
The Early Show
CBS This morning
Face the Nation
The Tonight Show
The Rush Limbaugh Radio Talk show

Ten days after the published worldwide
release of this book, we will be submitting a
Press Release to about 40,000 Journalists
nationwide, specializing in: Media, health,
news events, and other public interest topics.

I need your help to spread the word!

This is what happens when you have bad eyes, and drive at night without your glasses. I scratched the left side of my car on the wall of the parking garage one evening, when coming home from a late dinner with my girl friend.

The author would like to express his Thanks to:

President Obama and First Lady Mrs. Obama

Hillary Clinton

Vice President Joe Biden

The entire Obama Administration and Staff

Blue Shield Health Insurance

Ana Robles – Surgery Coordinator at Ophthamology Associates of the Valley

Manijeh Kasher, Tick Tock Insurance

Freedom Vision Center, Encino, CA

Dr. Brad Elkins, MD
Eye Surgeon Extraordinaire

INTRODUCTION

Last year my office took a six month leave of absence. I went through some hardships, recovered. Started over, worked hard, got back on my feet again, found a new office, started three new companies from scratch and made it through my 17th tax season.

I wrote and published six books and started moving forward again this year with a new outlook on life, new office, luckily I have my health and hundreds of clients came back.

We've serviced 4,000 clients in the past nine years! Hundreds of client references.

Seventeen years ago, I started my first practice as an Accountant, bookkeeper, Tax Preparer and document preparer in the San Francisco Bay Area, where I grew up and went to College, Golden Gate University School of Accounting -- started the practice from scratch, built it up, then started a second practice in Seattle, WA and several years later after getting married and having a daughter, moved the offices down to Los Angeles, CA.

I'm also a screenwriter, producer, film maker and have made two Travel documentary films, and also just started my own Hollywood Production company this year in May.

I'm re-energizing a feature length screenplay I wrote ten years ago, after making a 20 minute short film DVD condensed version that was shown at the New York Short Film Festival to a sold out audience and packed house.

By the end of this year we will have ten independent feature film projects slated for development. I'm also a writer and published author.

In December, I re-activated my document preparation, business consulting and Incorporation services practice, and this year in January 2014, I formed Moshe Publications, Inc. I'm Publisher and editor in chief.

We've published six books so far: (Four Biographies and two books are "how to" business guides) and this is my seventh book published, to be released and distributed beginning next month -- worldwide.

I'm also a single weekend dad with a beautiful 14 year old daughter, Molly. Family and kids come first.

I've built up my current practice from scratch over the past nine years in Los Angeles, mostly from client referrals. We've added many available services to our list, including Tax Settlements and Resolutions, inquiry removals and credit repair services, Non profit filings, LLC filings, and Incorporations.

Over the years, I've helped over 200 people to prepare, and file their non profit, everything from women's shelters, dog rescue foundations, children's youth groups, musical foundations, ministries, churches, synagogues, and high school GED programs -- ALL APPROVED -- 100% for non profit tax exempt 501c3 status.

I've gained enough experience to expedite the non profit process to under 90 days; it used to take eight months or longer.

I'm also an avid golfer, tennis player, and biker and love to travel.

Growing up, I used to play golf every chance I got. Me and my brother Rick would go and play in the school yard early in the morning on the weekend and have our own make shift golf course with flags etc.

I used to go every year to Hawaii after Tax season, and in 2007 took my daughter with me to Maui, and in September 2008, I took Molly with me to Turtle Bay Resort on the north shore of Oahu for seven days, to celebrate her ninth birthday and I got to play two rounds of golf on one of the most beautiful golf courses you've ever seen. Hawaii has some of the best and most challenging courses in the world. The challenge comes from having the ocean in the background and such beautiful scenery, with a slight breeze, it can all be very distracting to the average golfer. For me it was paradise.

Unfortunately, the last time I got to go to Hawaii was in 2008 before an ordeal that I had to go through and then my eyesight deteriorated gradually from cataracts disease, making it not only harder to play golf, but to work and enjoy life.

I've serviced over 4,000 clients over the past nine years, including 300 annual tax return clients, and I've helped dozens of people get caught up and back in compliance with their taxes.

Even with my eyesight worsening over the recent years, I never gave up my love of golf, racket ball, traveling, and movies. I'm 48 years old as I write this book.

Being a hard working small business owner myself I've gained some valuable knowledge and experience over the years, and I'm very flexible and understanding as to what self employed people and small business owners need done and what challenges there are running a business, making payroll and getting health insurance is sometimes on the bottom of people's priority list.

In this book my argument is: why everyone, not just some, everyone should obtain The Obama Care Affordable Health insurance, especially if you're a small business owner, self employed, or a 1099 Independent contractor.

It's not easy creating and building something from scratch to support your family. But in my opinion, it's worth it. The rewards outweigh the hardships and difficulties we encounter.

Of course your health and family come first, and it's very important to have a good stable business or venture to support your family -- with the ultimate goal of having a full time successful and prosperous business!

We also do business plans, executive summaries, P & L reports, projections, back taxes, amended taxes, payroll forms, income and expense reports, Balance sheets, Corporate taxes and Secretary of State re-instatements if needed, corporate credit build up services, business Trade vendors, rapid credit builder programs, personal and business loans and lines of credit, signature loans (I have three lenders that I'm working with currently).

I even prepare Bankruptcy filings once in a while and divorce forms for clients in need.

200 non profits -- all approved. 700 Incorporations. 300 annual Tax clients.

Hundreds of client references. 500 Corporate consulting and accounting clients, 600 Wage garnishments and Tax liens stopped.

4,000 clients serviced nationwide in the past nine years!

I can't fix the past, all I can do is work hard to make the future better, with a different approach, loyal employees, better services, and better customer service and follow up. Employees and customers/clients are what makes a business what it is.

I've acquired and developed a unique set of powerful skills that makes me a valuable asset in the small business arena.

I can be on the phone with two or three agencies at once, talking with the State Tax department for a client on one line, stopping a wage garnishment, while on the other phone at the same time, speaking with the IRS on behalf of the same client, stopping collection letters and a bank levy -- and have both calls end successfully.

I'm an entrepreneur -- have been my entire adult life. Self-employed business owner.

Creating exciting and new business services, ideas and practices. Building businesses from scratch.

Even in college, I had my own Janitorial and Window Cleaning business -- working on mansions every weekend -- three houses every weekend turned into at least $600-700, enough to put gas in the car, buy school text books and pay for lunches on school days. I hired a part time assistant at $10 an hour, if the job was too big for just me (this was twenty five years ago).

I quoted the price to each home owner by counting up the windows and determining how many hours the job would take.

I also created and built up a children's entertainment birthday party magic show balloon twisting business, with audience participation, live bunny, choreographed to Disney music etc -- I became so well known in the children's birthday party business in my early 20's, doing four or five shows at birthday parties every weekend, I was working from just referrals for a couple years; one mom told another mom, etc -- I was booked solid every weekend for months in advance… this was all before starting my second Seattle Accounting Tax practice in 1993-94.

We know one thing for sure: Business owners provide local jobs and create opportunities.

Let's make things happen this year!

Randy

Best Regards, Randy

My poor vision began to look like the photos on the right over the past eight years. I had advanced stages of cataracts disease. But since I was self employed, and a single weekend dad paying child support, I couldn't afford to get the health insurance I needed to pay for medical services, etc.

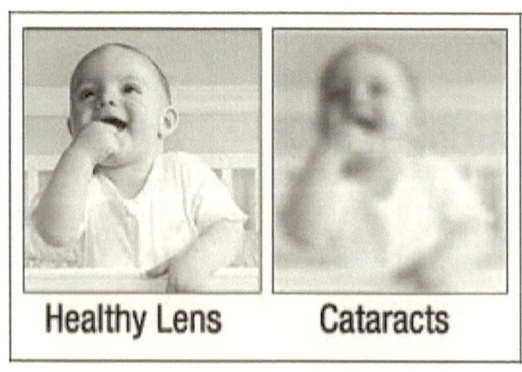

Healthy Lens   Cataracts

Normal vision   Vision through a cataract

IMPORTANT STATISTICS

Before I tell you my personal story, you should be made aware of a few statistics that I recently discovered after doing some research on Google, while I was writing my latest book:

How many people are currently residents of the US? The **United States population** on July 4, 2013 was: 316,148,990 ... This includes **people** whose usual residence is in the 50 states and the District of Columbia

How many Insurance Agents are there in the U.S? Per the U.S. Bureau of Labor Statistics:

"Insurance sales agents held about 434,800 jobs in 2008. About 51 percent of insurance sales agents work for insurance agencies and brokerages"

How many self-employed people are there in the U.S? The U.S. has an estimated 20 million self-employed people. That's 6.6 percent of all reported jobs, but down from a high of 7.2 percent in 2006. This includes people that receive a 1099 as an Independent Contractor.

This is according to a new report from CareerBuilder and Economic Modeling Specialists Intl. (EMSI). Self-employment grew rapidly from 2001-2006, adding close to 1.8 million new jobs nationwide. Since the beginning of the recession, however, self-employed jobs declined by 936,000 and did not recover post-recession.

Self-employed workers are those who, when surveyed by the U.S. Census Bureau, consider self-employment to be a significant part of their income or time working.

Owners of incorporated business are not counted among the self-employed nor are workers who freelance or have other smaller, secondary sources of income.

If they're not including incorporated businesses in that total I would add another 5-10 million, because I know from experience that most small business owners eventually incorporate, which makes them "an employee" of their own company, which in my opinion, is still kind of self employed. They work for themselves, and pay themselves (when they can).

"The market for self-employment was significantly weakened by the recession. However, as full-time employment in traditional workplaces continues to improve we expect entrepreneurial opportunities to follow suit with time," said Matt Ferguson, CEO of Career Builder and co-author of _The Talent Equation_. "A rebound in housing will lead to more growth for independently employed construction and real estate workers as well as other occupations in the supply chain. Moreover, many high-paying jobs in IT and consulting have already seen positive self-employment growth in recent years."

Key Findings

• Self-employment jobs have declined 5 percent since 2009. Since the peak of self-employment in 2006, the U.S. has lost nearly a million self-employed jobs, a 9 percent decline. By contrast, the number of jobs for salaried employees – those who work in traditional work settings – has risen 4 percent since 2009.

• The decline in self-employed jobs coincides with a rise in Americans working on the side to supplement their incomes. More people are getting second and third jobs, but fewer people are dropping their day jobs altogether to work on their own. According to a new CareerBuilder survey, 20 percent of full-time workers picked up a second job in 2013 or plan to do so in 2014.

• The biggest declines in self-employment have come in agriculture, real estate, child care, and retail trade industries. While self-employment for construction laborers has grown since 2006, the industry as a whole has experienced significant declines. The biggest gains in self-employment have been in lower-wage jobs – landscaping workers, maids, personal care aides and photographers.

• Even with low-wage occupations at the top of the self-employment growth list, several high-wage occupations have made significant gains, most notably market research analysts/specialists, management analysts, and computer occupations such as web developers.

• Nearly two-thirds of self-employed jobs in the U.S. are taken up by men (62 percent), and more than 30 percent of the self-employed are 55 years and older.

• Only North Dakota and Washington, D.C. have seen self-employment increases since 2009, and their gains have been minimal (5 percent and 1 percent, respectively). Among large metros, only five have seen at least 2 percent growth in self-employment jobs: Memphis (4 percent), Bridgeport-Stamford-Norwalk (3 percent), Austin (2 percent), Orlando (2 percent), and Las Vegas (2 percent).

How many Independent Contractors (1099) are there in the U.S? Over 10 million.

How many small business owners are there with 0-5 employees? In 2010 there were 27.9 million small businesses.

If there's an estimated 27.9 million small businesses in our country and estimated 10 million self employed people wouldn't that make the total number of people either self employed, or 1099 Independent contractors or small business owners, incorporated or not incorporated add up to almost 40 million people?

I'm not sure if they're including in their statistics the difference between self employed, independent contractors and small business owners, but needless to say, it's a good percentage of folks who don't have health insurance offered to them through a regular full time W2 job at a medium size or larger company.

How many golfers are there in the US?

Historical Data

According to the National Golf Foundation, there were 28.8 million golfers in the U.S. in 2000, 30 million in 2005 and 29.5 million in 2007.

Decreasing Numbers

The number of golfers from 2007 to 2008 dropped by about 3 percent due to a struggling economy. Most of the decrease can be attributed to those golfers who were playing less or not at all.

How many Self employed Accountants do we have in the US: There are 1,300,000 Accountants, CPAs and Auditors in the U.S. currently.

Almost half of all Accountants are considered self employed, work more than 40 hours a week and experience very long hours, especially during tax season. I would like to find out how many of these self employed Accountants and Tax preparers as well, don't have any insurance currently.

How many people have some form of eye disease (cataracts, glaucoma)?

How many people in the U.S. have cataracts?

A: Cataract affects nearly 22 million Americans age 40 and older. By age 80, more than half of all Americans have cataracts. Direct medical costs for cataract treatment are estimated at $6.8 billion annually. [Source: Vision Problems in the U.S.: Prevalence of Adult Vision Impairment and Age-Related Eye Disease in America.

How many people in the U.S. have glaucoma?

A: Glaucoma affects almost 2.3 million Americans age 40 and older.
[Source: Vision Problems in the U.S.: Prevalence of Adult Vision Impairment and Age-Related Eye Disease in America. Prevent Blindness America and the National Eye Institute, 2008.

How many people in the U.S. suffer eye injuries each year?

A: Each year more than 2.5 million eye injuries occur and 50,000 people permanently lose part or all of their vision. Ninety percent (90%) of all eye injuries can be prevented by using protective eyewear.
[Source: United States Eye Injury Registry summary report, 1998-2002]

Who is most likely to be injured?

A: Nearly half (47.6 percent) of all eye injuries occur in people 18 to 45 years of age.

A: Males are at greater risk in all age groups: 73 percent of eye injuries occur in males.
[Source: United States Eye Injury Registry summary report, 1998-2002]

Q: Where do most eye injuries occur?

A: Nearly half (44.1 percent) happen in the home.

A: 14.7 percent of eye injuries occur during sports; among children age 5 to 14, this is the most common form of eye injury. Most could be prevented through use of appropriate protective eyewear. [Source: United States Eye Injury Registry summary report, 1998-2002]

How many part time or full time employees are there in the U.S. that work for a small business that does not offer any health benefits?

The small business economy includes 6 million businesses and 21.7 million self-employed people. Both groups are at a disadvantage in the healthcare marketplace—small firms can't get the same health plan discounts as can large firms. And the self-employed are stuck in the individual insurance market with its higher costs and restrictions on applicants with any history of illness.

This information is outdated because with the current Obama Care Affordable Insurance and protecting Patients Act, everyone must be accepted for Health Insurance.

The data show that small businesses pay more than large ones:
• Firms with 1 to 9 workers (the vast majority of small businesses) paid adjusted premiums 18% higher than those paid by firms

with 1,000 or more workers, according to a 2006 study supported by the Commonwealth Fund.

- They also pay more in administrative costs—27% of premiums for very small firms, compared with 9% for businesses of at least 100 employees, the Congressional Budget Office estimates.

Small business health insurance premiums have risen 113% over nine years, a growth rate of nearly 9% annually, according to Kaiser Family Foundation surveys.

Many uninsured people work for a small employer.

These higher costs make it harder for small firms to provide insurance, which is why the smaller the firm, the less likely it is to provide health insurance.

- 99% of large firms offer healthcare coverage, while 78% of firms with 10 to 24 workers offer coverage; that drops down to just 49% among firms with fewer than 10 workers, the Kaiser Family Foundation has found.
- The percent of smaller employers offering health plans has declined over time as premiums have risen-it dropped from 57% in 2000 to 49% in 2008, the Kaiser survey said.

These trends mean that many of the uninsured are employed but work for small companies that don't offer coverage:

- Of the 45 million uninsured Americans in 2007, 22.3 million (about half) were self-employed or worked for small businesses, say Employee Benefit Research Institute estimates.

The economy relies on small businesses' vibrancy.

- Of the 142 million people working in the private sector, 42% work for themselves or for businesses with fewer than 100 employees.
- In a healthy economy, small businesses create 75% of net new jobs. When the economy is recovering from a recession, small firms play an even greater role in job creation, responsible for all new positions.
- Small businesses have trouble attracting talented employees-or don't get started in the first place—because people can't afford to leave jobs that provide health insurance, a phenomenon economists call "job lock."

How many people filed Bankruptcy last year partially because of medical bills they couldn't pay from hospital stays, surgeries, etc?

For the year 2011, 1.37 million people filed bankruptcy, which was less than the 1.55 million people who filed bankruptcy in 2010.

A significant percentage of bankruptcies are caused by medical debt, so one might think that states with the highest filing rates would have the highest percentage of uninsured. This is not so. States with low bankruptcy filing rates, such as Texas, South Carolina and Alaska have significantly higher percentages of uninsured than do the states with the highest bankruptcy filing rate.

How many people paid cash for a doctor's visit last year, without insurance? A significant number of doctors are now accepting cash patients, but I don't have the exact number.

Eventually ALL people without insurance will need to go see a doctor, and that's why this is such a timely and important subject.

How many people in the U. S. have had a cataracts surgery procedure and lense implant in the past five years: Over 6 million.

How many people in the U.S. don't have Health Insurance? About 44 million people in this country have no health insurance, and another 38 million have inadequate health insurance. This means that nearly one-third of Americans face each day without the security of knowing that, if and when they need it, medical care is available to them and their families.

I have a feeling that these numbers are low, based on my research. I'm guessing over 100 million people in this country, especially self employed people, need to get insurance.

Having no health insurance also often means that people will postpone necessary care and forego preventive care - such as childhood immunizations and routine check-ups-completely.

Because the uninsured usually have no regular doctor and limited access to prescription medications, they are more likely to be hospitalized for health conditions that could have been avoided.

Delaying care for fear of medical bills is a downward spiral that leads to ultimately higher health care costs for all of us. More than one third of uninsured adults reported they have problems paying their bills, which helps explain why many of the uninsured don't seek out the care they need until the last minute.

But when an uninsured person is in crisis and cannot pay, that burden falls upon the insured population, the hospitals, the doctors and the government. And these billions of dollars of "uncompensated care" drive up health insurance premiums for everyone.

How many people are taking advantage of the Obama Care Affordable Insurance, as of the writing of this book, so far?

Before the open enrollment period began in October of last year (2013) to sign up for coverage, the Obama administration was confident 7 million Americans would sign up.

CHAPTER ONE

AN EMAIL I WROTE TO SEVERAL CLIENTS ON JUNE 25th, 2014

After four years of waiting and suffering, my Obama Health care Insurance coverage -- Blue Shield California covered plan finally kicked in, I was given full coverage on April 15th of this year (the last day of Tax Season) which kicked in May 1st, and I'm now scheduled for the miraculous and life changing cataracts surgery procedure on my right eye this Thursday morning!

They will remove the advanced cataracts disease and insert a brand new bionic Lense in my right eye restoring my poor blurry vision and 50% loss of eyesight, to near perfect far sighted vision...

I was afflicted young - and diagnosed over twenty years ago with advancing stages of cataracts in both eyes, but was told at the time by the eye doctor that I wouldn't have to worry for years.

Years passed and my eye sight got worse as the cataracts disease spread into thousands of tiny dots and scars in both eyes, causing a 50% loss of vision quality. I paid over $5K cash for my left eye in 2010, but it was so cost prohibitive, and I couldn't afford to spend over $700 a month for Health Insurance (if I was even accepted for coverage with a pre existing high blood pressure condition and being a smoker), with so many other important things and overhead to cover, including office rent, salaries and wages and child support, the right eye never got done and I went SEVEN years without any Health Insurance coverage.

The Obama Care Affordable Health Insurance Blue Shield covered California Plan is covering 70% of the surgery $3,800), and 80% of the Doctor's visits $300, physical exams to get cleared for the surgery, the anesthesiologist $800+, the prescription eye drops are an extra $150 needed and the Surgery Center Facility (four hours approx) which is well over an additional $2,000 all together: $5,800 total --- **and Blue Shield Health insurance is covering 80%!**

It's a Blessing and I'm so grateful and excited.

I'll be at home recovering and healing Thursday afternoon and hopefully right back to work Friday.

I'm writing a new book, about how the Obama care plan helped me and my family, enabled me to get coverage and I'm dedicating the book to the Obama Administration and Hillary Clinton and Blue Shield Insurance -- written especially for ALL the Self employed people and small business owners in this country in their 20's-60's who have no Health insurance currently.

The plan works! Even for 48 year old white Jewish guys like me with a small business and family to support.

I can't wait to spread the word!
Proposed Title of my newest Book:

A Very Special Thanks to the Obama Administration, Hillary Clinton, Blue Shield Insurance and Dr. Brad Elkins, Eye Surgeon

By Randolph M. Hirsch, The Golfing Accountant

The miraculous story of how the Obama Health care phenomenon enabled one small business owner, weekend dad to get Health Insurance coverage and get the cataracts eye surgery he needed.

A touching, Important and very Informative book: WRITTEN ESPECIALLY FOR ALL SELF EMPLOYED PEOPLE AND SMALL BUSINESS OWNERS ACROSS THE COUNTRY WHO CURRENTLY DON'T HAVE ANY HEALTH INSURANCE COVERAGE.

TARGET MARKETS FOR MY BOOK:

Self-employed people across this great country of ours

Small business owners in the USA

Independent Insurance Agents all across our country wanting to offer the Obama Care Health plan and insurance coverage to their self employed clients -- During the open enrollment period starting in July through October 15th of this year.

Any part-time or full-time employees who work for small business owners that don't offer any Health Insurance benefits

Golfers and Accountants Nationwide who are interested in Affordable Health Insurance coverage!

Anyone who has had a recent medical scare or procedure, didn't have any insurance -- and does not want to go through anything like that again --- without proper Insurance!

Any person who suffers from cataracts disease but cannot afford the costly surgery because of lack of proper health insurance coverage, and continues to go without a necessary medical procedure for lack of knowledge what benefits there are out there.

Everyone has an opinion about Obama Care, and their own situation, I realize that -- But I'm here to tell you first hand -- it helped me get the necessary eye surgery that I needed for years and years.... Otherwise I wouldn't have any coverage and would have waited and suffered with poor vision for at least another year or two, until I was almost blind.

Best Regards, Randy

P.S. My upcoming Newest Book is scheduled for completion and publishing in July, and will be released and distributed worldwide, under my publishing company's banner, through Amazon, EBAY, Barnes and Noble, Borders, Kindle, Nook, and at least a hundred (or more) Independent online book sellers worldwide.

I need your help to get this book distributed to the masses.

CHAPTER TWO

Cataract

From Wikipedia, the free encyclopedia

Cataract
Classification and external resources

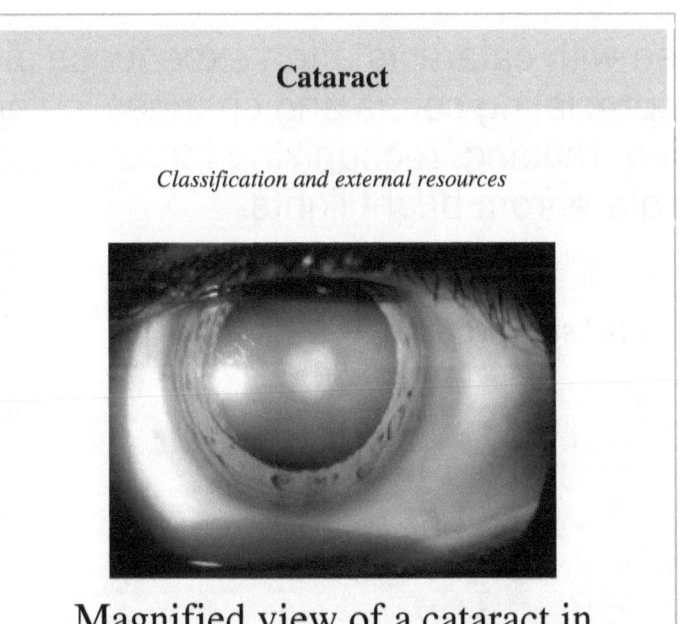

Magnified view of a cataract in
a human eye, seen on examination with
a slit lamp using diffuse illumination

A **cataract** is a clouding of the lens inside
the eye which leads to a decrease in vision. It
is the most common cause of blindness and is
conventionally treated with surgery. Visual loss
occurs because opacification of the lens
obstructs light from passing and being focused
on to the retina at the back of the eye.

It is most commonly due to aging but there are many other causes. Over time, yellow-brown pigment is deposited in the lens and this, together with disruption of the lens fibers, reduces the transmission of light and leads to visual problems.

Those with cataracts often experience difficulty in appreciating colors and changes in contrast, driving, reading, recognizing faces, and coping with glare from bright lights.

Signs and symptoms

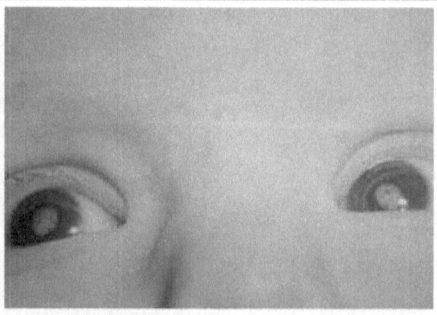

Bilateral cataracts in an infant due to congenital rubella syndrome

Signs and symptoms vary depending on the type of cataract, though there is considerable overlap. People with nuclear sclerotic or brunescent cataracts often notice areduction of vision. Those with posterior subcapsular cataracts usually complain of glare as their major symptom.

The severity of cataract formation, assuming that no other eye disease is present, is judged primarily by visual acuity test. The appropriateness of surgery depends on a patient's particular functional and visual needs and other risk factors, all of which may vary widely.

Age

Age is the most common cause. Lens proteins denature and degrade over time and this process is accelerated by diseases such as diabetes and hypertension. Environmental factors including toxins, radiation and UV light have a cumulative effect over time. These effects are worsened by the loss of protective and restorative mechanisms due to alterations in gene expression and chemical processes within the eye.

Trauma

Blunt trauma causes swelling, thickening and whitening of the lens fibers. While the swelling normally resolves with time, the white color may remain. In severe blunt trauma, or injuries which penetrate the eye, the capsule in which the lens sits can be damaged. This allows water from other parts of the eye to rapidly enter the lens leading to swelling and then whitening, obstructing light from reaching the

retina at the back of the eye.
Following electrical injuries, cataracts may develop in 0.7 to 8%.

Radiation

Ultraviolet light, specifically UV-B, has been shown to cause cataracts and there is some evidence that sunglasses worn at an early age can slow its development in later life. The lens filters UV light; so once that is removed via surgery, one may be able to see UV light.It has also been recognized, from experimental animal studies and epidemiological studies in humans, that microwaves can cause cataracts. The mechanism is unclear but may include changes in heat sensitive enzymes that normally protect cell proteins in the lens. Another mechanism that has been advanced is direct damage to the lens from pressure waves induced in the aqueous humor. Cataracts have also been associated with ionizing radiation such as X-rays. In addition to the mechanisms already mentioned, the addition of damage to the DNA of the lens cells has been considered. Finally, electric and heat injuries denature and whiten the lens itself as a result of direct protein coagulation. This is the same process that makes the clear albumin of an egg become white and opaque after cooking. Cataracts of this type are often seen in glass blowers and furnace workers. See Glassblower's cataract.

Lasers of sufficient power output are known to damage the eyes and skin. Also see Laser safety.

Genetics

The genetic component is strong in the development of cataracts, most commonly through mechanisms that protect and maintain the lens. The presence of cataracts in childhood or early life can occasionally be due to a particular syndrome.

Skin diseases

The skin and the lens have the same embryological origin and can be affected by similar diseases. Those with Atopic dermatitis and Eczema will occasionally develop shield ulcers cataracts. Ichthyosis is an autosomal recessive disorder associated with cuneiform cataracts and nuclear sclerosis. Basal-cell nevus and Pemphigus have similar associations.

Drug use

Cigarette smoking has been shown to double the rate of nuclear sclerotic cataracts and triple the rate of posterior subcapsular cataracts. There is conflicting evidence over the effect of alcohol. Some surveys have shown a link, but others that have followed patients over time have not.

Medications

Some drugs, such as corticosteroids, can induce cataract development. Patients with schizophrenia often have risk factors for lens opacities (such as Diabetes, hypertension and poor nutrition) but it is unlikely that antipsychotic medications contribute to cataract formation.

CHAPTER THREE

Here's an email correspondence from one of my "difficult" clients that I received right after I got home from my cataracts surgery procedure on June 26th and June 27th:

Randy, ObamaCare is a government controlled, forced plan that will drive this country into the gutter. You've been suckered my friend.

Don't believe this evil regime of Liberals.

MY RESPONSE:

HI GREG: The cataracts surgery went very well yesterday -- it was successful. Thank God for Obama Health Care Blue Shield Covered Health Insurance!

As you know, they covered 80% and Obama Health care made it possible and affordable for me as a small business owner, to get the life changing procedure done.

My eyes have already improved 1000%!

Colors are more vivid and images clearer and crisper, I actually was able to see street signs while driving myself to the eye doctors this morning without glasses.

I'm home recovering and healing today and I can appreciate that you're waiting for the final $100 per client -- only one has shown me their credit reports so far, Harold Miller.

Unfortunately today I'm home, and have no office appointments or clients until Monday, early next week. I expect by that time, to have updates from the other four clients as well as copies of their recent credit reports, if they can pull the tri merge for me, after posting.

Take care and have a GREAT weekend!

THEN HE WROTE BACK:

Randy,

You're the VERY FIRST person I have EVER spoken to that actually

1)   Likes Obama Care and

2)   Found a doctor who will take it!

Nobody here back east really like him or OB Care. Gov't run health care is ANTI-CONSTITUTIONAL.
Myself, I won't touch it with a ten foot pole as I am sure it has a ton of strings attached. I'll stick to private pay!
That guy is a demonic, communist, Constitution shredding dictator wanna-be if ever I saw one!
I'm Def NOT A FAN...as you can tell. I'm a conservative guy ALL the way.

Private health care and competition in the market place, has served our country well for many

Years and we need to return to it pronto, in my opinion! Privatize health care and keep the gov't out of it
It would be even cheaper for us businessmen!

Anyway keep me posted on your clients reports, and I will look to hear from
you Monday.
Have a great weekend!

Later, Greg

P.s. I am starting a new Day Job Mon July 7th working a CAD job about a 30 minutes drive North for me. So will be doing this stuff nights & weekends at that point.

THEN I WROTE HIM BACK:

All the doctors and eye surgeons in America are jumping aboard now as fast as they can. It's a miracle and a blessing.

They won't cover 100% only 70-80% something called a co-pay deductible.

I'm so grateful and excited.

My latest book will be released next month to a worldwide audience.

I'm Already receiving invitations and requests for appearances, speeches and book signings. It's phenomenal!

I can tell you first hand it works! Obama Care Blue Shield Health insurance Covered California saved my life and my vision!

Best Regards, Randy

P.S. I will send you a signed copy when my new book hits the presses next month sometime, and an extra copy for your mom. What a miracle!!

P.S.S. It is private pay, optional and voluntary. I have a $262 monthly insurance premium. I'm sure even an intelligent self employed guy like you can appreciate $262 a month for full coverage.

It's already paid for itself ten times over with my eye surgery, physical exam, anesthesiologist, prescriptions and follow up exams total: $6K. Cost me around $1,500 out of pocket.

I ALMOST PUT THIS IN MY EMAIL TO HIM:

I could care less about your new job or your half an hour drive north.

My Suggestion: Get your head out of your ASS!

CHAPTER FOUR

Twenty five years ago in 1989, when I was 23 years old, I went to see the eye doctor for my routine annual exam. The eye doctor informed me I had something called cataracts disease in both eyes, but I wouldn't have to worry about it for years, until I was much older.

I asked my mom, Gail, what that could have been caused by and she said maybe an infection from a public swimming pool when you were five years old that went untreated.

Of course I would discover years later that there are many things that may have caused the cataracts to accelerate, including hyper-tension, diabetes in the family, stress, drug use and smoking.

I've had plenty of stress in my life this past several years, smoked a pack of cigarettes a day off and on for twenty years, and had hypertension that was treated for a while, then stopped. So I probably caused the cataracts disease to worsen on my own over the years. But wouldn't realize it until my mid 40's.

It wasn't until 2004, when I was 38 years old, that I would really need glasses. My eyes had worsened recently, I had just moved to Los Angeles from Seattle, WA with my little family, had a five year old daughter, and had to go register at the DMV for my new drivers license, and that meant taking the eye test before they issued the new license to me.

Well that was a disaster. I failed the eye test miserably. The DMV woman laughed me right out of the place. I passed the written test of course, 99% correct, but the eye exam – I couldn't even see the letters. I had been walking around for a year in a daze, everything blurry even back then in 2003-2004 my eyes had already started to give me trouble.

"Go get some glasses young man and come back." The DMv employee who tested me that day said.

I immediately went to a local eye doctor's office, got tested, and received my first prescription for contact lenses. I wore contacts for the next nine years.

The reason I had dragged my family down to Los Angeles was I had written a romantic character driven emotional comedy drama entitled "Once In A Lifetime: "Just Go For It!" A feature length screenplay about becoming a step dad and a group of friends in Los Angeles and how their lives all crossed paths over the course of a year. Since my ex wife Jennifer's parents both lived in Los Angeles, it wasn't too hard to convince her to uproot the family and move down there.

I eventually went through a divorce and became a weekend dad.

One Saturday in April 2006, at the Vine Street office during tax season, when Molly was about six years old and I brought her with me to the office for a full day of tax client meetings and appointments.

During tax season, people appreciate Saturday appointment openings because it was a day off from their jobs to get their taxes done. I'd already built up a good-sized tax practice by now.

I want to emphasize how important this next incident was in my life. Being a single weekend dad isn't easy, and being a self-employed business owner, building a practice and a business from scratch, isn't easy either. But everything I'm about to relate really happened. Some of you have been through similar experiences, even worse experiences; difficult times, suffering and hardship, and some of you may not have any relatable experiences at all.

Maybe you've never been a parent or a single dad, or owned your own business, or God forbid, been a self-employed tax accountant and tax preparer such as myself!

On that Saturday with Molly, the clients streamed in, one after another, back to back appointments all day long; starting at 8 a.m. Molly was very well-behaved and patient. I had her playing on the computer at first, and then switched her to watching a *Sponge Bob Square pants* DVD on the portable DVD player I had gotten her for her birthday the year before.

Noon came and went, and she was getting hungry and tired, but I didn't have any breaks scheduled or time set aside in between appointments. I just kept working and working, straight through, 1, 2, 3 p.m. Back-to-back meetings. Finally, around 3:30, I needed to use the restroom down the hall for a few minutes. I came back after a short time, maybe five or ten minutes, and Molly was face down on the floor, passed out on the ground, no pillow or blanket. She was just out cold. I continued to look at her for several minutes just lying there. It was a sad picture for me, and I'll never forget it.

I began to think to myself, why did I have to drag my dear Molly on the weekend with me to the office all day? I only had her every other weekend for God sakes. This was my precious time with her. From Friday night after I picked her up from the Carroll Rees Academy, until Monday morning when I dropped her back off. This was our precious, valuable time together, and you can't get that time back again.

I would forever remember that day, and made a promise to the both of us that if I ever had to bring her to the office with me again, it would only be for an hour or two at the most, and only if absolutely necessary. She deserved my undivided attention.

CHAPTER FIVE

April 11th, 2014: I had a very painful swelling in my lower back. It turned out to be the same exact cyst I had twenty five years earlier in college. It re-surfaced, swelled up with infection and I could barely sit down.

But without health insurance I was scared to death that a doctor's visit would cost me a fortune.

I searched on Yelp for a good dermatologist in the area and made an appointment at Dr. Milton Kaplan's office in Tarzana, CA.

After filling out some paperwork, they took me into a room where the nurse told me to undress. Then Dr. Kaplan walked in and had me lay down on the table face down.

He took a three inch syringe and injected it right into the cyst, it was excruciating. Then he lanced it with a scalpel.

I don't know if I was more scared about the procedure or the doctor's office bill afterwards. I didn't have any insurance. I thought for sure this would cost me $700-$800-$900. The secretary told the Dr. I was a "cash paying customer" and they only charged me $250 that day. I also had to go get a prescription anti-biotic after, and that ran about $80.

This was the straw that broke the camels back.

What if the visit had cost $1,000 or more.

What if the next time I get sick or have to have something done it requires an overnight stay in the hospital, or more serious surgery that would cost tens of thousands?

I needed health insurance! Was there anything available for a 48 year old self employed guy like me?

On April 15th, 2014, four days later, I contacted the Insurance agent that was recommended to me by Amir, my girlfriend's brother. It was the last day for enrollment in the Affordable Care Act program during this open enrollment period.

Just for the heck of it, as a long shot, I took a chance and submitted my application. They based their decision and what my insurance rates would be on last year's income and my current income this year. In 2013 I worked for the first seven months and during the last five months of the year, after my office closure and devastating hardships, had no income, so my total annual income for the previous year was much lower than in previous years, adding to my stress and financial difficulties.

My net profits as of April 15th, 2014 year to date, from my consulting, document preparation and Incorporation services practice, combined with my full-time income from the Web Sites company, was only $3,200 a month at the time of the application.

I was approved for full insurance coverage at a monthly premium of $262 a month!

The first monthly premium came due on May 1st and that's when my insurance coverage began.

A few days later, I received a thick packet in the mail and my insurance card was enclosed. I was so excited to have insurance again after all these years.

I stuck that insurance card into my wallet and it felt so good that day.

Then about five letters came in the mail welcoming me to Blue Shield and confirming my Health insurance policy coverage.

That's when the miracles started to happen.

After seven years without any insurance, I'd suffered with poor and blurry vision and it got worse and worse as the years went by.

Four years earlier in 2010 I had saved up enough to have the left eye operated on and paid over $4K cash at the time.

I never expected to be able to afford another costly procedure on the right eye, and the cost for the surgery and for the surgery center, had gone up to almost $6K since then, if you include the doctor's physical exam to get cleared for the surgery, the anesthesiologist and prescription anti biotic eye drops needed after the surgery.

The surgery seemed so far out of reach for me, especially after the ordeal I had gone through over the past year or so.

My office was closed, lost my home, took my daughter out of school, lost my phone services, clients, furniture put in storage, my business – all gone. Scattered to the winds. Had to start from scratch.

I made an appointment with Dr. Brad Elkins's office coordinator, Ana Robles, for an examination.
I took another chance, maybe part of the cataracts surgery would be covered? Couldn't hurt to ask. The worst they could say was no. First, I called Blue Shield Insurance and was transferred to five different departments from customer service to sales, and couldn't get a straight answer.

One person said "No the cataracts surgery was not covered."

Another person said "Yes the surgery would be covered. I needed to find out for myself.

I hoped that at the eye surgeon's office, Ophthamology Associates of The Valley, they would be able to exam my eye, make a diagnosis, I knew how bad the eyesight was, but they would also be able to contact Blue Shield hopefully, enter my membership policy number in their computers and give me a realistic answer and expectation.

Initially, the billing person at the eye doctor's office said "NO we don't accept Obama Care."

But Ana, the surgery coordinator gave me the best news I had heard in years that day.

CHAPTER SIX

"It looks like Blue Shield Covered California Insurance will cover 70% of the surgery, and 80% of the anesthesiologist (Around $800), 80% of the surgery center (Usually $2,000).

"Your out of pocket cost will be $1,000 to the surgeon and $400 to the surgery center."

I replied "What's the next available date about a month from now that you can schedule me for the cataracts surgery?"

Ana responded "How's June 26th?"

"Yes! Sign me up. Schedule me immediately. I'm in. Let's do this!!"

I couldn't believe my ears. Since that day, I was so grateful and excited. I was finally going to get the life changing and miraculous eye surgery that I had so desperately needed for so long. My eyes had gotten so bad recently; I was walking around in a blurry fog.

I met with Dr. Elkins right after my meeting with Ana. He said this to me after I told him I had been approved and accepted through the Obama Care Affordable Insurance Act for Blue Shield Insurance and that was what was enabling me to schedule my much needed cataracts surgery.

"You're the perfect example of how it CAN work and obviously it does work."

Colors were dull; I couldn't play a round of golf without contact lenses or the clunky glasses I wear at the office or for driving. Without glasses, I could not read street signs anymore.

When I got my physical exam two weeks later at Dr. Kirsch's office in Sherman Oaks, he told me I had hypertension and would need to take a pill. He gave me a prescription. I took it over the Walgreen's in Tarzana, and the usual $80 prescription pill cost me $4 bucks with the insurance.

The physical exam which is normally $300 including X-Rays, MRI, blood pressure test, blood and urine analysis, was only a $ 45 Co-pay!

This Insurance was saving me money every which way. After the surgery, it will have paid for itself ten times over already – and I was only covered for two months...

Miraculous! What a Blessing.

Me and my daughter Molly during happier times, I took her to Hawaii for her ninth birthday, September 2008, before the cataracts really destroyed my eyesight.

I didn't get the left eye done until October 2010 and had to pay cash for that surgery.

My daughter and I in San Francisco right after my brother Rick's wedding ceremony, March 2010, seven months before my first cataracts surgery.

Molly with our little doggie Bijou at the house in Sherman Oaks, CA before the cataracts surgeries or my devastating ordeal that caused me to have to start all over again.

I would eventually lose my house to foreclosure, my business, office, everything.

As my eyes worsened, I began to worry and suffer daily – how long could I go without a needed medical procedure?

The Insurance companies were quoting me outrageous monthly premiums due to my pre-existing condition, and I was a smoker which didn't help either.

I went seven years from 2007-2014 without any health insurance coverage: Until the Obama Care Affordable Insurance Act finally helped me!

At Madame Tussaud's Wax Museum, with a
perfect replica of President Obama, in New
York City, May 2009. My girl friend and I got to
visit NYC for five days, right after my ordeal.
Wish I could really meet him in person to say
Thanks, but I have to take what I can get ☺

CHAPTER SEVEN

A year and a half later I would pay $5K cash to get the left eye operated on. My eyesight was already getting bad, but it worsened over the years until I could barely see.

I realize that cataracts surgery is a fairly simple and routine procedure these days and sixty million people have had it done.

It was affecting my work, my driving, my enjoyment of life, my ability to get things done. I couldn't afford the surgery, because of my hardships and difficulties, the office closure the year before, the struggles with child support for my daughter, office rents, salaries and wages, etc. I didn't have any health insurance coverage, and couldn't afford to get any insurance for seven years!

This is how my vision looked for the months and years leading up to my second cataracts surgery procedure in the right eye on June 26th, 2014.

No this is not a mis-print, this is how I saw everything from my eyes.

What It's Like

This is how a street scene looks with normal vision.

This is how the same scene looks with cataracts.

Lift the fog & clear the blur.

Normal vision

Vision through
a cataract

Intraocular Lens Implant

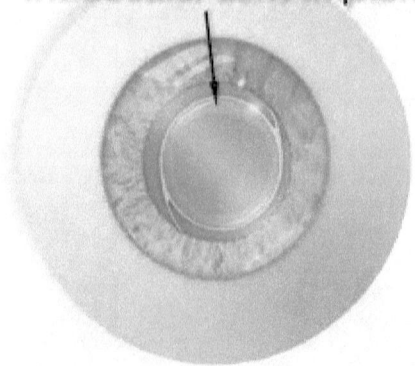

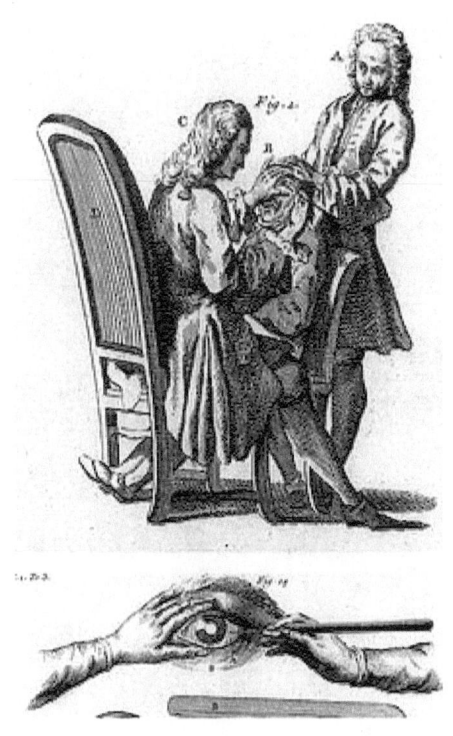

A cataract surgery. *Dictionnaire Universel de Médecine* (1746-1748).

MODERN NO-STITCH CATARACT SURGERY

Advanced Cataract Surgery

Based upon the results of your recent eye examination, your doctor has determined that you have a cataract. Although it's a condition that requires surgery in which the cataract will be removed, having a cataract is nothing to be overly alarmed about. You probably have many questions regarding the procedure and what options you have available. This brochure will help to shed some light on the procedure that will start you on your way to improved vision.

What is a cataract?

A cataract is a clouding of the normally clear, natural crystalline lens in your eye. This clouding is usually due to the aging process but can also be caused by eye trauma, heredity, diabetes, and even some medications. Whatever the cause, cataracts typically result in blurred or fuzzy vision and sensitivity to light.

Cataract formations occur at different rates and can affect one or both of your eyes at the same time. Fortunately, with modern medical technology, your cataract can be treated safely and effectively through a microsurgical technique. In fact, cataract surgery is one of the most successful surgical procedures performed today-about 95% of all cataract surgeries result in an improvement in vision.

Normal Vision   Cataract Impaired Vision

Photos courtesy of Alcon Labs., Inc.

The best way to treat your cataract is to remove the cloudy lens and replace it with a new, clear artificial lens. This can be accomplished two ways. The first technique, called extracapsular cataract extraction (ECCE), involves removing the cloudy lens in one piece. This technique requires a large incision of 10 to 12 millimeters
in length.

The second technique is the latest advance in cataract removal. It's called phacoemulsification, or phaco.

Phaco Probe
Photo courtesy of Alcon Labs., Inc.

In phaco surgery, a small ultrasonic probe is inserted into the eye. This probe breaks (emulsifies) the cloudy lens into tiny pieces and gently sucks (aspirates) those pieces out of the eye. Phaco requires a small incision of only 2.75 millimeters or less. Your surgeon will determine which method is most appropriate for your condition.

Whichever technique is used to remove your cataract, anesthesia will be a necessary part of the procedure. Two types of anesthesia, local or topical, are used in most cataract cases.

Anesthesia

Local anesthesia eliminates any sensation of pain and prevents movement of the eye during surgery. Topical anesthesia is administered by placing drops on your eye. It eliminates any sensation of pain but does not prevent your eye from moving around. Both types of anesthesia leave you fully awake and aware during the operation. The type of anesthesia that the surgeon will choose for you will depend on the technique your surgeon chooses and the condition of your eye.

Incision

In order to remove the cataract and replace it with a new lens, your doctor will make an incision in your eye. Where the incision is made and how large it will be depends on the technique (ECCE or phaco) your surgeon chooses for you.

Incisions can be made in either of two places in your eye-clear cornea or the sclera. The cornea is the transparent area of your eye over the iris and pupil. The sclera is often referred to as the white part of your eye.

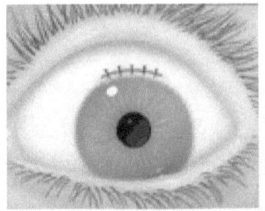 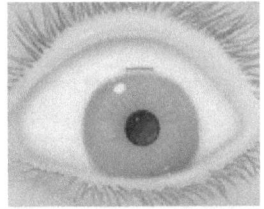

6 mm Conventional Incision   2.75 mm Advanced Incision

Photos courtesy of Alcon Labs., Inc.

The ECCE removal technique requires a large incision in the sclera. The phaco technique requires a smaller incision in either the sclera or clear cornea. Smaller incisions usually result in little discomfort during or after surgery, often do not require stitches, can aid in reducing astigmatism, and may provide a faster postoperative recovery period.

Replacement Lenses

Once the cataract removal part of the procedure is completed, your doctor will have to replace it with a permanent, artificial lens called an intraocular lens, or IOL.

There are two types of IOLs available-nonfoldable and foldable. Nonfoldable lenses are made of PMMA, a hard plastic material first used as an IOL in 1979. Foldable lenses are made of either silicone or acrylic.

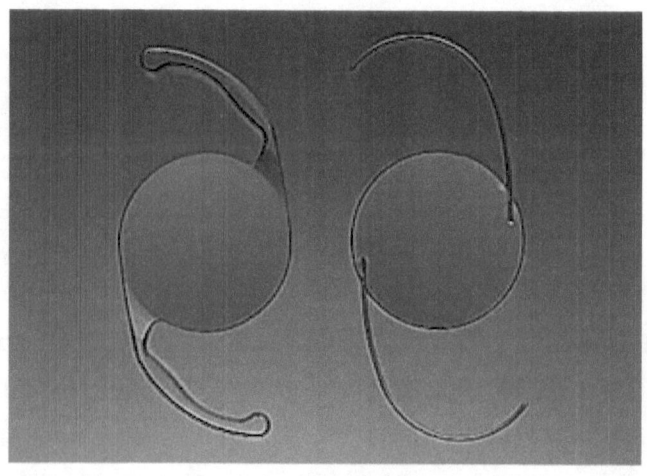

Nonfoldable and foldable IOLs
Photo courtesy of Alcon Labs., Inc.

With the recent advance of foldable IOLs, lenses can be implanted through the same small incision that is created in the phaco procedure. These IOLs are made of a flexible material allowing them to be folded for implantation. Once inside the eye, the lens unfolds and returns to its original shape. Several different IOL materials are available today.

The latest advance in foldable IOLs are the ACRYSOF? Acrylic Foldable Intraocular Lens, Staar Surgical Collimer lens, Several foldable Toric lenses to treat astigmatism, and AMO Rezoom multifocal and Alcon RESTOR multifocal. ACRYSOF is made of an inert material that is very compatible with eye tissue.

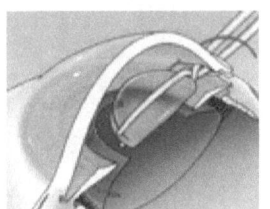 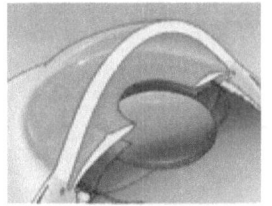

Folded IOL In Incision   Unfolded IOL In The Eye

Photos courtesy of Alcon Labs., Inc.

Toric IOLs and LIMBAL RELAXING INCISIONS can correct astigmatism. You can talk to either Dr. John or Patrick Costello about your astigmatism and how it can be dealt with during cataract surgery to decrease your dependence on spectacles.

See our section on multifocal lenses on the Procedures and Services page to find out more about this type of lens implant.

After Your Surgery

One of the benefits of today's small incision cataract procedures is that you will be able to return home soon after your surgery. When your procedure is complete, your doctor may or may not apply a patch over your eye. Before you leave, you will be given instructions on how to care for your eye, including information on any medications that may be required. You should be able to resume your normal activities shortly after your surgery.

In time, improvement in your vision will continue as your eye recuperates from surgery. Your doctor will schedule follow-up appointments, as needed, to check on your visual recovery progress.

Your Future Vision

Today, advancements in small incision surgery provide you with the most effective method of restoring your vision in the treatment of cataracts. Your doctor uses the latest state-of-the-art techniques, equipment, and intraocular lenses to provide you with a safe, fast and effective outcome.

- The improvement in your vision will not only enhance your normal lifestyle and activities, it will also add years of enjoyment to your life. You've got a lot to look forward to!

Then my right eye worsened even more... I would cover my left eye and everything was very blurry. This is how my right eye saw things the days and weeks leading up to the second cataracts surgery:

This is how it looked driving without my glasses

One day before my cataracts surgery I went back to the eye doctor's office to make my final cash deductible co-payment of $400.

The total out of pocket cost to the surgeon was $1,300 all together which included some additional tests, and a special device used during the surgery to help the doctor with exact measurements and placements of the lense implant and the follow up post operative exam. Another $439 out of pocket went to the surgery center.

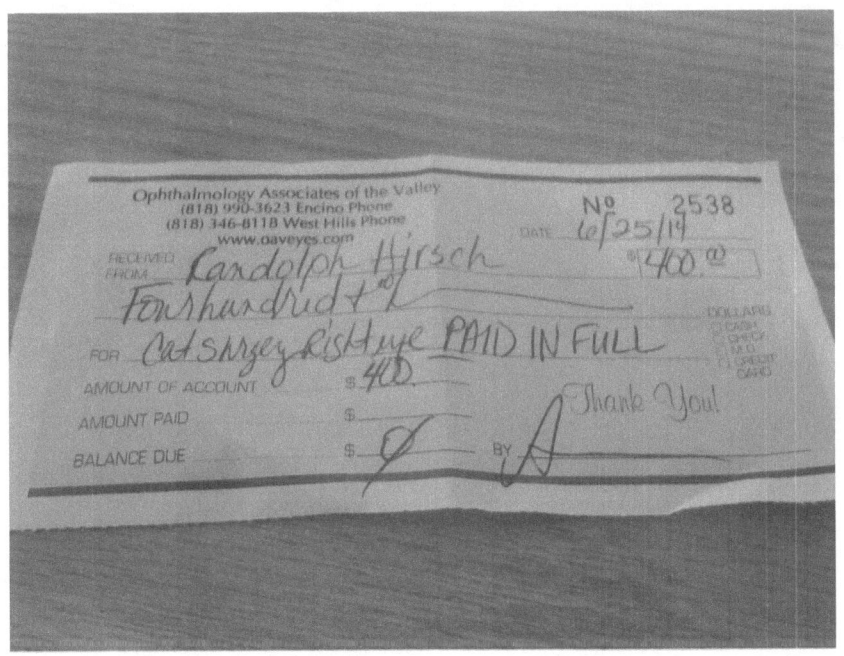

The sweetest words I heard that day were from Ana the surgery coordinator as I put the four one hundred dollar bills on her desk to complete my required payments.

I had been coming in for the past month or so, since that first meeting and examination, and paying whatever I could, $200 one week, $300 cash the next, etc.

"Well you're done. You're paid in full." She said to me.

"Remember to take your prescription eye drops three times a day, and we will see you at

6:30 am tomorrow morning at the Freedom Vision Surgery Center. Then the day after you'll be back here at 8:30 am for your post operation exam with the doctor."

"Thanks so very much Ana. See you Friday." I replied.

I walked out of her office with a sigh of relief and went home to prepare for the surgery the next morning.

I would wake up at 5 am, and wasn't allowed to eat or drink anything because they would administer anesthesia to relax me before and during the procedure.

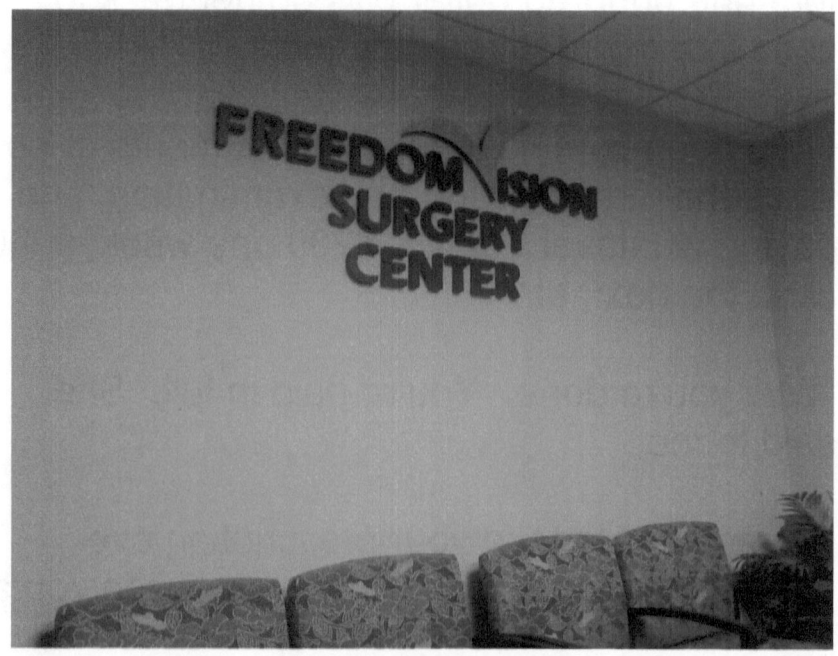

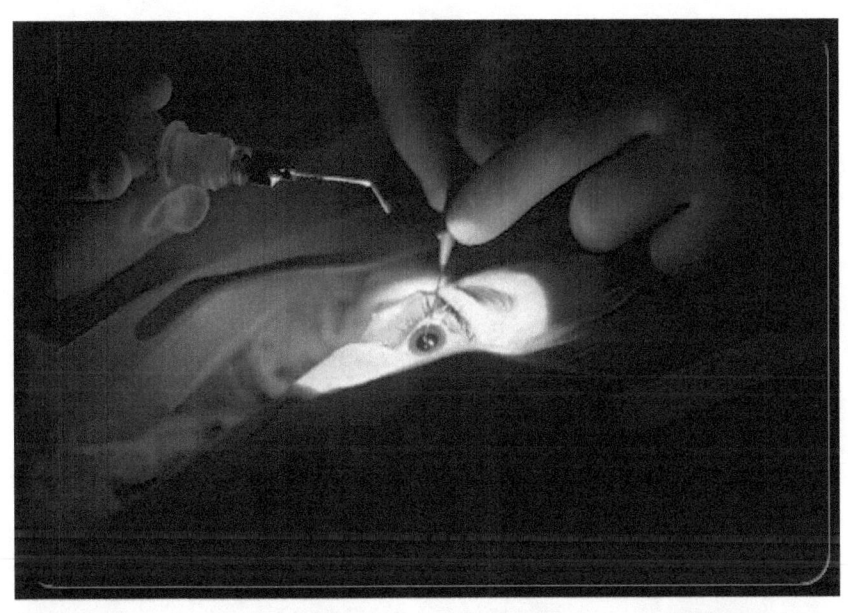

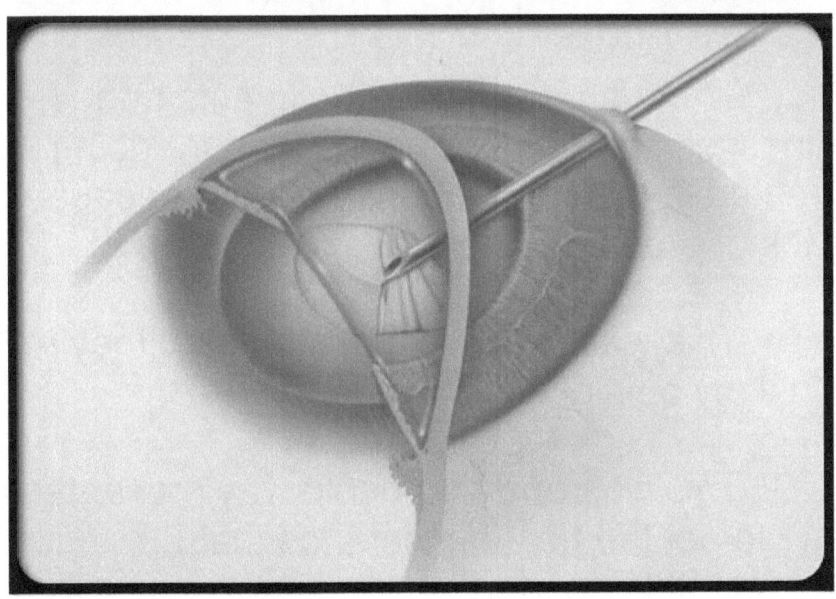

89

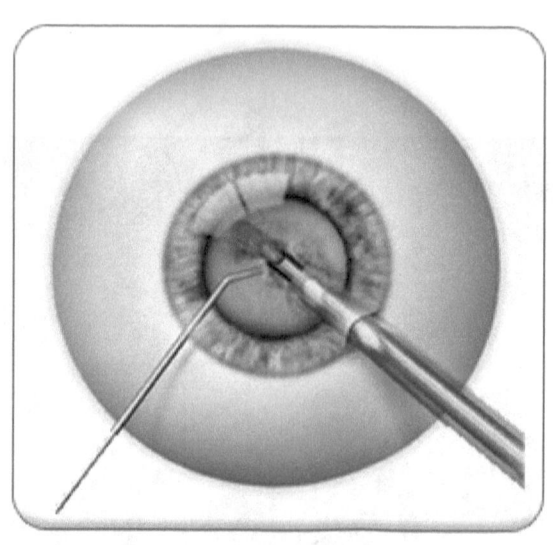

CONCLUSION

There are many other ailments and illnesses and medical needs that are going untreated in this great country of ours because of lack of proper insurance.

This was my personal story and they're only my opinions.

This was one affordable way presented to me to get the health insurance that I desperately needed.

People need insurance – period. Get it any way you can -- as soon as possible.

The day before the miraculous and life changing surgery, I placed my hand over my left eye several times to just look out my right eye. At street signs, trees, the TV, flowers, people, driving, all around me – I wanted to remember how blurry it was that day, so that I would never ever forget how bad it was for my eyes, and what a miracle I was about to be granted. If everything hadn't happened just as it did, I would probably have gone without Health Insurance coverage for maybe another year or two, and suffered with my vision impairments indefinitely.

If I hadn't had the cyst removal procedure on April 11th at Dr. Kaplan's office, the dermatologist – without insurance coverage, which prompted me to get insurance four days later.

If I hadn't called and emailed Amir to ask for a referral.

If Manijeh with Tick Tock Insurance hadn't contacted me on April 15th, the last day of open enrollment. If she hadn't gotten my application submitted and approved in time.

If Blue Shield Covered California Insurance had not accepted me or started my coverage on May 1st.

If I hadn't thought to call and go back to Ophthalmology Associates of the Valley and been examined by their staff and Dr. Elkins and scheduled with Ana.

If Blue Shield had refused to cover the costly and necessary surgical procedure, or if they didn't cover Obama Care Affordable Blue Shield covered California Insurance, none of this would have happened or been possible.

I'm writing this book with my new eyes.

Thanks to: Dr. Brad Elkins, Eye Surgeon with Ophtamalogy Associates of the Valley in Encino, CA; Ana their wonderful surgery coordinator, Blue Shield Health Insurance Covered California; Manijeh with Tick Tock Insurance, the insurance agent who helped me to get the Affordable Health insurance; Amir, my girl friend's brother, for referring me to her; Secretary of State Hillary Clinton, for being so pro active in the Health Insurance arena; Vice president Joe Biden; and a very special Thanks to President and Mrs. Obama, and their administration and staff – and all of the hard working and caring people that helped me to get approved for Health Insurance when I really needed it.

I have my eye sight restored thanks to the Affordable Health Insurance Act and Dr. Brad Elkins! Life is Beautiful again.

Thanks Mr. Obama! Thanks Dr. Elkins!

This will sure help my golf game too!

This is how clearly I can see now:

I can actually see the golf balls after I hit them without squinting and searching all over the fairway!

The very first weekend after my cataracts surgery, I went to play at the Brookside Golf Country Club in Pasadena, right next to the Rose Bowl.

I could actually see the golf balls on the fairway.

I didn't lose very many balls – and I can't blame my golf game on my poor eyesight anymore! ☺

VALUABLE INFORMATION AND REFERENCES

http://www.hhs.gov/healthcare/rights/

https://www.healthcare.gov/

http://en.wikipedia.org/wiki/Patient_Protection_and_Affordable_Care_Act

http://www.whitehouse.gov/healthreform

http://www.nei.nih.gov/

For special guest appearances, speeches and book signings, contact Randy through Moshe Publications, Inc.
Toll-free: (855) 333-6897 or (818) 908-4083
Email: MoshePublications@gmail.com

ABOUT THE AUTHOR

Randolph M. Hirsch began his writing career in 2004 with his first feature length screenplay, Once In A Lifetime: "Just Go For It!" A Romantic comedy drama. He eventually condensed the screenplay in to a 20 minute short film, which he later produced and submitted it to the New York short film Festival, and it was very well received.

Following that, he made two Travel Documentary films in 2006 and 2007, Randolph Hirsch Discovers Ukraine and Randolph Hirsch Discovers Paris.

He later released a how to business guide for Accountants entitled: The Blueprints Marketing Guide for Accountants, Tax Professionals and CPAs.

Recently, Mr. Hirsch has released six books in 2014: There's A Reason You're Here Moshe; Once In A Lifetime: Just Go For It! The feature screenplay; Daniel Day-Lewis, three time Academy Award Winning Best Actor, the Ultimate Biography; Philip Seymour Hoffman, Academy Award winning Actor of Capote and the Master, the Ultimate Biography of a Great Actor; Matthew McConaughey, Best Actor

2014: The Ultimate Biography; and Making Kids Smile, a how to guide for aspiring children's entertainers and performers.

He is also re-releasing a newly re-mastered DVD version of his short film, Once In A Lifetime: Just Go For It, just as it played at the New York Short Film Festival ten years ago. He's currently finishing "The Boogie Nights Series." A Complete color photo Biography series of books about the director, Paul Thomas Anderson and his favorite actors and actresses from the film Boogie Nights, including Mark Wahlberg, Don Cheadle, Julianne Moore, William H. Macy, Burt Reynolds and Heather Graham, due to be released in August, 2014.

Mr. Hirsch has just begun a five book series covering these topics: The power of Social Media, Twitter, Facebook, Kindle, Google and SEO Marketing.

With the release on July 4th, 2014 of A Very Special Thanks... he has dedicated the next year of his life to promoting the Obama Care Affordable Insurance and Protecting Patients Act and Blue Shield Covered California, for the life changing miracle they gave him.

With the recent completion of Randolph Hirsch's four latest books, all released in September 2014: Quit Smoking: "How I finally did it after thirty years and You Will Too!" Molly and Dad's Grand Hawaii Adventure, a children's story and picture book. The Roy Yamaguchi story: International Chef and founder of Roy's Hawaiian Fusion Restaurants. "The

Ultimate Biography and color photo tour of Roy's Restaurants, including the six in Hawaii." Seth McFarlane: The Ultimate Trivia Guide and Biography of "The Family Guy," Randy is now developing his new Film Production Company, Los Angeles-International Films, Inc. and spends his time with his family, as well as preparing for his upcoming first independent feature film production, slated for development and pre-production in 2015.

Randy lives in Los Angeles with his fiancée, his beautiful daughter and their little doggie Bijou.